IN FOCUS: NATIVE AMERICANS

HOPI

HISTORY AND CULTURE

MARK STEWART

Cavendish Square

Published in 2026 by Cavendish Square Publishing, LLC
2544 Clinton Street, Buffalo, NY 14224

Website: cavendishsq.com

Portions of this work were originally authored by Ivy Kuszewski and published as *Hopi* (Spotlight on Native Americans). All new material this edition authored by Mark Stewart.

Publisher: Katie Kawa
Book Design: Lisa Miley

Portions of this work were reviewed by: Robert J. Conley, Former Sequoyah Distinguished Professor at Western Carolina University and Director of Native American Studies at Morningside College and Montana State University.

Photo Credits: Rich Reid (4); William Henry Jackson/Detroit Publishing Co. (5*); Library of Congress (6 top*, 7*, 16*, 20*); Promking (6 bottom); Frederic Remington (9*); Peter Newark's American Pictures (10, 13 top, 20, 23); NY Public Library/Underwood & Underwood (11*); Bettman Archives/Getty Images ((12); Museum of the American Indian (13 bottom*); Thomas McMullin & David Walker (15*); C.C. Pierce/ Doheny Memorial Library (18*); Detroit Publishing Co. (19*, 21*); U.S. Department of the Interior (22); JKinnor/Wikimedia Commons (23); Time & Life Pictures (25); Corbis (26); Robert Alexander/Getty Images (28); Freepik.com (29).

Cover images (clockwise from top: Author's Collection; Robert Alexander/Getty Images; Getty Museum Open Content Program*; Mary Evans/Picture Library Ltd; Art Institute of Chicago*; Underwood & Underwood Publishers*.

*These images are in the public domain.

Cataloging-in-Publication Data
Names: Stewart, Mark, 1960 July 7-.
Title: Hopi history and culture / Mark Stewart.
Description: Buffalo, NY : Cavendish Square Publishing, 2026. | Series: In focus: Native Americans | Includes glossary and index.
Identifiers: ISBN 9781502675002 (pbk.) | ISBN 9781502675019 (library bound) | ISBN 9781502675026 (ebook)
Subjects: LCSH: Hopi Indians--History--Juvenile literature. | Hopi Indians--Social life and customs--Juvenile literature. | Indians of North America--Arizona--History--Juvenile literature. | Indigenous peoples--Social life and customs--Juvenile literature.
Classification: LCC E99.H7 S94 2026 | DDC 979.1004'97458--dc23

CPSIA compliance information: Batch #CS26CSQ: For further information contact Cavendish Square Publishing LLC at 1-877-980-4450.
Printed in the United States of America

CONTENTS

ABOUT OUR GLOSSARY

In this book, there may be several words or terms you are reading for the first time, or words that are familiar but used in an unusual way. All of these words appear in **bold type** throughout the book and are defined on page 30.

I AM THE LAND

The mesas of the American Southwest are among the most spectacular landscapes on earth. Over the course of millions of years, rivers and streams cut through wide **plateaus** to create large, elevated platforms with 360-degree views of the surrounding land. Some mesas cover 100 square miles (260 sq km) or more. The Hopi people built their culture around these dramatic geological features for many centuries, constructing **adobe** villages atop the mesas' steep slopes and farming the valleys surrounding them.

A Hopi farmer tends to his corn crop. Hopi agriculture made the most of every drop of rainwater.

The Hopis are the westernmost of the **Puebloan** people. Their ancestors moved south from the "four corners" region, where the states of New Mexico, Colorado, Utah, and Arizona meet. The Hopi people live on a reservation in Arizona that is a mile (1.6 km) or more above **sea level**. This elevation contributes to a dry, **arid** climate that demands expert management of water resources, because rainfall is limited to 5 inches (13 cm) a year at the lower elevations and 15 inches (38 cm) at the higher elevations. That expertise dates back many centuries; the Hopi village of Oraibi is the oldest surviving settlement in the United States at over 850 years old.

The mesas of the American Southwest were formed over millions of years by ancient streams and rivers.

A Hopi village performs a ritual called the Harvest Dance. Spiritual life remains a central part of tribal culture.

Hopi farmers successfully **cultivated** corn, beans, and squash in their semi-desert environment. These three plants—which are sometimes called the "Three Sisters"—create a **complete protein**, which sustained the strength of the Hopis for more than 1,000 years. Agriculture enabled the tribe to create permanent settlements, in contrast with many of its neighbors, such as the Navajos. Some of the terraces Hopi farmers plant today have been used for centuries. The Hopis took advantage of other resources, including large and small game, wood from juniper and pinyon forests, and coal for heating, cooking, and firing of pottery. This connection to the land has played an important role in the spiritual life of the Hopi people.

Each Hopi village saw to the safety and security of its own people. The concept of private property did not exist; different **clans** owned the fields along the waterways below the settlements. Members of a Hopi clan traced their ancestry back through the kinship of mothers, all the way back to an original ancestor. Today there are more than 30 clans—including the Cloud, Spider, Snake, Bear, Butterfly, and Eagle clans. At one time, there were more than 70. Because all members of a clan are considered "family," Hopi men and women are not allowed to marry members of their own clan.

According to Hopi beliefs, the First World of time and space was created by the sun spirit Tawa. The creatures there evolved as they entered the Second and Third World, and then emerged through a large opening into the Fourth World as humans. Their guide was Spider Grandmother.

Each Hopi clan has its own spirit being, called a kachina. Kachinas play specific roles in village celebrations and spiritual ceremonies.

◀ The village of Oraibi has been occupied since at least the 1200s.

FIRST CONTACT

In 1540, Spanish explorer Francisco Vázquez de Coronado set out from Mexico in search of gold. In 1541, one of his captains, Pedro de Tovar, split off to explore lands to the west. He encountered the Hopis, who refused to allow his soldiers to pass through their territory. After a brief fight, during which several warriors were killed, the Hopis made peace and agreed to recognize the King of Spain. When it became clear that the tribe did not possess any gold, however, the Spanish moved on.

Starting in the 1600s, Spain began establishing **missions** in the region where the Hopi people lived. Missionaries wanted to convert them to Christianity. This effort met with some success, but most Hopis held on to their traditional beliefs. They did, however, trade with the missions to acquire metal tools, livestock, and new plants. Unfortunately, this contact enabled European diseases to sweep through Hopi villages, where people lived close to

This painting shows the arrival of Spanish soldiers in the 1500s.

one another and had no immunity to **smallpox** and other illnesses.

Christianity did appeal to some Hopis, who lived in and around the missions that the Spanish built in their villages. This created a divide within the tribe that sometimes turned violent. In 1700, traditional Hopis attacked tribe members who had **converted** in the village of Awatovi. Awatovi was completely destroyed and was never reoccupied.

I AM A WARRIOR

The Hopi have long been known as the "peaceful ones." But to keep the peace, a tribe needs warriors who are capable of defending their land and people. Hopi raids and attacks against their neighbors were rare; their weapons tended to be for hunting first and fighting second. Their creative and resourceful craftsmen were skilled at making both.

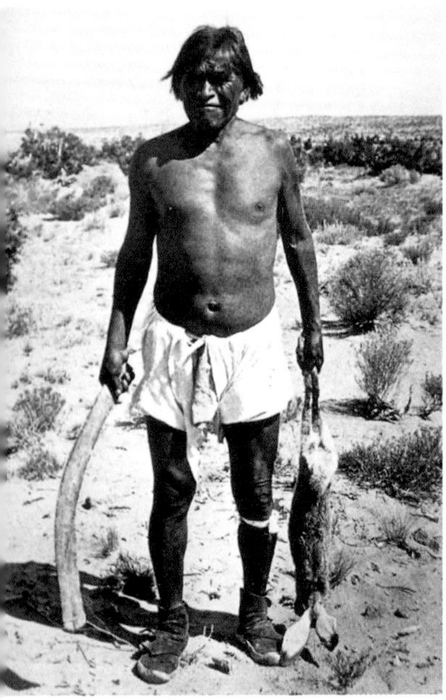

A Hopi hunter holds his throwing stick in one hand and his dinner in another. Throwing sticks doubled as weapons in battle.

The Hopi weapon of choice was the throwing stick. With practice, a warrior could stun or kill his target with amazing accuracy. Like the throwing stick, the war axe could be used as both a tool and a weapon. The Hopi longbow could propel arrows great distances, while the Hopi spear—which was tipped with a razor-

Hopi warriors were familiar with every inch of their landscape, which made them expert defenders.

sharp stone point—was also an effective killing weapon. It was thrown using an **atlatl**, a device that increased a spear's speed and accuracy. All these weapons were also beautifully decorated for use in rituals and ceremonies.

Beginning in the late 1600s, the Navajo people came into conflict with the Hopis. The Navajo were under pressure from Spanish settlers and began moving into Hopi territory. In addition to using Hopi resources, such as water and grazing land, Navajo warriors launched raids against Hopi villages. Hopi war chiefs and warriors used their experience as hunters to become skilled defenders. The two tribes battled on and off until they moved onto

government reservations in the 1860s.

As masters of their environment, the Hopis used the landscape to create an "early warning" system that included lookouts and natural barriers. Hopi warriors detected their enemies from miles away, long before they reached a village. During attacks on Hopi settlements, raiders encountered defensive architecture that made success unlikely.

▲ Hopi homes were built for defense. They were only accessible by ladders.

The kachina that best represents the Hopi warrior is Chaveyo. If a person was causing problems in a Hopi village, a war chief might call on one of his men to dress as Chaveyo and confront the offender. According to tribal legend, Chaveyo led Hopi warriors during the Pueblo Revolt against the Spanish in 1680. They killed a priest and destroyed the church and mission at the village of Oraibi. Chaveyo still participates in many rituals, including the traditional Bear Dance.

◀ This photo from 1880 shows a Hopi warrior on horseback on the lookout for enemy raiders. The Hopis developed an effective early-warning system for village defense.

A NEW REALITY

In 1821, Mexico won its independence from Spain and controlled Hopi territory until 1848, when the United States defeated Mexican forces in a war. The Mexican government did not have much contact with the Hopi people before that. This would not be the case with the Americans.

In 1850, Chief Nakwaiyamtewa and six Hopi tribal leaders traveled to Santa Fe to meet with James Calhoun, the Indian Agent in charge of New Mexico. They sought (and received) protection against the Navajos.

In the years that followed, the Hopis began to accept certain aspects of American culture, including some Christian and **Mormon** religious practices. Hopi chiefs visited Washington, D.C., and met with President Chester A. Arthur. They were very impressed with the city. In 1882, the Arthur administration established a reservation for the Hopis which amounted to about one-tenth of their traditional land.

Indian Agent James Calhoun was the official representative of the American government.

Five years later, in 1887, the government began forcing Hopi children to attend a boarding school in Keams Canyon, on the eastern edge of the reservation. The goal of the school was to strip away their Native culture. Also in 1887, Congress passed the Dawes Act, which promoted the concept of individual land ownership and divided reservation land into small **parcels**. On the Hopi reservation, the law destroyed traditional farming practices, which greatly depended on **communal** land water rights.

BEING HOPI

The origin of the name of the Hopi is unknown. It is translated in various ways, including "the peaceful people" and "one who behaves." They have always seen themselves as caretakers of their environment. They believed their religious ceremonies benefitted the entire world. The concept of the "Hopi Way" brings together notions of spirituality, good manners, and respect for all things—and still touches every aspect of Hopi life.

For example, the division of labor between Hopi women and men differed from other tribes. While Hopi men were responsible for hunting and village defense, they also contributed to a wide range of household chores,

Two young Hopi women grind corn into flour that could be used for making piki.

The Hopi people have always believed that their religious ceremonies benefitted the whole world.

as well as farming. Men also handled most of the weaving and carving duties, including the making of kachina dolls.

Hopi women were involved in all aspects of food production. They ground corn and cooked meals. One of the most common foods was called piki, a paper-thin bread made of blue corn that was cooked on a special hot stone found in every Hopi household. Women were also responsible for creating pottery, which was used for cooking and storage. They also played a key spiritual role in Hopi society.

Children also held a special place in Hopi society. Families hid their babies from the sun for the first 19 days of their lives. On the 20th day, a baby's grandmother named it in a family ceremony. The baby was then blessed with cornmeal and taken outside to meet the sun at dawn. Hopi children were initiated into a society at age seven, when they received new names. They learned how to do things by helping their parents with daily tasks and listened to stories that helped them understand the meaning of the Hopi Way.

When girls were ready to marry, they participated in a corn-grinding ceremony and put their hair up into

a special "squash-blossom" style over their ears, which they wore until they were wed. Boys began participating fully in ceremonial life between the ages of 16 and 20. At that time they were initiated into one of four societies: Singer, Horn, Agave, or Wuwuchim. Agave is a desert plant cultivated by the Hopis, which provides food, fiber, and **fermented** drinks. Wuwuchim is a ceremony that marks the beginning of a new ceremonial year.

Each Hopi village was independent and governed itself. Typically, the village chief (*kikmongwi*) chose and trained the next leader, but the villagers had to approve the choice. Often, the head of the Bear Clan led a village—solving problems and disputes, and working with outsiders. The second-in-command, the village crier, called out the news and announcements as he walked through the village each morning.

◀ Hopi girls pose with their traditional squash-blossom hairstyle.

SOMETHING SACRED

In the arid lands occupied by the Hopi people, rain was, and still is, vitally important. Not surprisingly, much of ceremonial life was devoted to honoring and communicating with spirits, asking for life, good crop yields, and rain. Many ceremonies lasted for eight or more days. They began with secret rituals performed

Spiritual life found its way inside every Hopi home. This altar featured multiple religious symbols and could be accessed by a ladder.

in kivas and then moved into a central **plaza**, where the entire village could get involved. Kivas are sacred rooms, usually round and below ground level, where a number of activities take place.

Some spiritual ceremonies were strictly women's ceremonies, while others were social events for the entire village. The four Hopi societies staged ceremonies, but certain tasks were the responsibility of specific clan members. For example, a man of the Sand clan

◀ One of the most dramatic Hopi ceremonies is the Snake Dance. The dancers handled poisonous rattlesnakes.

◀ The legendary potter Nampeyo shows her work. She inspired generations of artists that followed her.

had to bring sand to make the altar in one ceremony. Ceremonies started when the village crier called everyone to gather. Many times, offerings of feathered prayer sticks, or *pahos*, were placed on altars and in other sacred places. Many of these ceremonies continue today, including the Snake Dance, a prayer for rain that involves the handling of live snakes. Snakes symbolize **fertility**, rain, and the forces of nature in Hopi society.

Today, nine different sacred ceremonies are typically performed by the Hopi people. Over the centuries, they have developed many layers of symbolism—so much so that an outside observer might find them difficult to understand. Also, there is great significance placed on making every word and action perfect. To make a mistake might bring misfortune to a village.

Not surprisingly, Hopi artistic life is closely connected to the history and spirituality of its people. Hopi pottery, for example, is among the most admired and sought-after in the world. This tradition was nearly lost when the Hopis began using machine-made pots. Nampeyo, a Hopi-Tewa woman born in 1860, began making clay pots using ancient designs and methods. She inspired many generations of Hopi artists.

Nampeyo's great-granddaughter, Dextra Quotskuyva *(left)*, brought great originality and creativity to her own work. So did Quotskuyva's daughter, Fannie Nampeyo. Quotskuyva's son, Dan Namingha, harnessed his creative energy as a painter and sculptor. His work explores the connections between the earthly and spiritual worlds, and includes many Hopi symbols. His sons, Arlo and Michael, are accomplished artists as well.

PAST, PRESENT, FUTURE

The Hopi reservation covers more than 2,500 square miles (6,500 sq km) in northeastern Arizona. The Hopi people live in villages atop three mesas: First Mesa, Second Mesa, and Third Mesa. Because the reservations are located in a remote area, they have had more success than other Native American groups in preserving their culture. According to the 2020 United States census, the reservation's population is about 8,000 people.

An artist working on the Second Mesa makes coiled baskets and trays for visitors to the reservation.

Mining on tribal lands produces income, but also threatens the environment. The Black Mesa coal mine provided jobs but also damaged sacred sites. It closed in 2005.

Although estimates vary, about that many people of Hopi descent live elsewhere in the United States.

The Hopi reservation is completely surrounded by the Navajo reservation. This led to a dispute over land that lasted for decades. In 1974, the Navajo-Hopi Settlement Act was passed to solve this problem, but only made it worse. The disputed land was split, with members of the two groups ordered to move to "their" side. This created a forced relocation of many Navajos and Hopis—an uncomfortable reminder of the troubles of the 1800s. Not until 2006 was this difficult situation finally resolved.

High among the challenges for the Hopi people is a weak economy. Tourism has been a controversial source of income. More than 100 years ago, the U.S. government hoped to boost the Hopi economy by encouraging visitors to witness their colorful ceremonies. The Hopi people felt it was disruptive to their culture then (and many still do). Another source of income, coal mining, is

also unpopular for the toll it takes on the environment and the possibility of an environmental disaster.

Women on the reservation have organized themselves to specialize in specific products. First Mesa women make pottery, Second Mesa women make trays and baskets from **yucca**, and Third Mesa women make trays and baskets from **wicker**. Hopi silver workers also make jewelry featuring traditional and modern designs. This work does not appeal to many young people, who choose instead to leave the reservation in search of steady jobs. Many join the U.S. military. This is a great concern to those who want to protect Hopi culture and traditions, including the Hopi language.

The greatest threat to the Hopi way of life is climate change. Because there are no rivers running through the reservation, they are almost entirely dependent on rainfall. For centuries, they have practiced dry farming of their most important crop, corn—a technique that relies on predictable rainfall and its runoff. Droughts have

◀ Hopi farmers face a new challenge in the form of climate change. It is a major threat to their way of life.

become more frequent and severe in recent years, which has been attributed to the planet's changing climate. Less rain not only translates into shorter growing seasons. It also means that less water reaches the underground springs that the Hopi also rely upon. The ability to adjust and respond to a tough environment has defined the Hopi people for centuries. If history teaches us anything, it is that they will find a way to survive and thrive.

Gaming has proved to be a good source of revenue for many Native American tribes. Although the Hopis would be allowed to open gambling casinos on their reservation, tribal leaders have refused to do so. They believe that it is not the Hopi Way.

◀ A Hopi girl competes in a Native American clothing contest in 2018. Responsibility for preserving tradition and culture is passed down from generation to generation.

GLOSSARY AND FURTHER READING

GLOSSARY

Adobe—A kind of clay used to make sun-dried bricks.

Arid—Having almost no rain.

Atlatl—A device attached to the bottom of a spear making it easier to throw.

Clans—Close-knit extended families related by kinship or common ancestors.

Communal—Shared by all members of a community.

Complete Protein—A protein that contains all nine amino acids the human body needs.

Converted—Adopted a new religion.

Cultivated—Raised crops.

Fermented—Changed to alcohol through the breakdown of sugars.

Fertility—The natural ability for people, plants, and animals to reproduce.

Missions—Religious outposts created to introduce Christianity to Native Americans.

Mormon—Part of a Christian movement started in the 1830s now known as the Church of Jesus Christ of Latter-day Saints.

Parcels—Units of land that can be bought and sold.

Plateaus—Large areas of level high ground.

Plaza—A public square or open space.

Puebloan—Native Americans who are descendants of the Ancestral Pueblo people, including Hopis and Navajos.

Sea Level—A measure used in calculating the elevation of a geographical feature.

Smallpox—A virus brought to the Americas by Europeans, for which Indigenous people had no natural immunity. By the mid-1800s, more than 75% of Native Americans may have died of the disease.

Wicker—Thin twigs that can be shaped into baskets and other household items.

Yucca—A plant in the agave family with fibers that are used to make household items, sandals, and clothing.

BOOKS

Krupat, Arnold. *Boarding School Voices: Carlisle Indian School Students Speak*. Lincoln, NE: University of Nebraska Press, 2021.

Rossiter, Brienna. *The Trail of Tears*. Mendota Heights, MN: North Star Editions, 2025.

Tyler, Ron. *Native Americans: The Complete Plates of McKenney, Catlin, and Bodmer*. Cologne, Germany: Taschen America, 2024.

Various Authors. *My Life: Growing Up Native in America*. New York, NY: MTV Books/Simon & Schuster Children's Publishing, 2024.

ABOUT THE AUTHOR

MARK STEWART has written more than 150 non-fiction books for educational publishers, covering history, sports, and popular culture. His family tree tells a complex story common to many Americans. Mark's ancestors include some of the first European colonists, as well as the Indigenous people with whom early settlers interacted. Some faced off on the field of battle while others fought side-by-side. His 10th great-grandfather was **Myles Standish**, an officer on the ***Mayflower***, while his ninth great-grandmother was **Singing Bird Corbison**, who was described as a "Shawnee woman" but who was probably from the **Wampanoag** tribe. The Wampanoag people saved Standish and his fellow **Pilgrims** from starvation during the winter of 1620–21, forming the basis for the story of Thanksgiving. The descendants of Corbison and Standish blended into a single family in 1789, and then headed west in search of opportunity. This brought Mark's ancestors into direct conflict with Native people along the frontier in the 1700s and 1800s. Mark's sixth great-grandmother recalled frantically casting bullets for her husband as they defended their small Kentucky fort from an attack. Another served under 23-year-old **Abraham Lincoln** in the Illinois Militia during the Black Hawk War of 1832. Mark's more recent ancestors chose to fight their battles with words—as writers and editors of books, newspapers, and magazines. In 2007, he authored a history of the **Indian Removal Act of 1830** and the infamous **Trail of Tears**.

INDEX